Short Walks in Auckland

Best of Central

By Helen Wenley and Grace Haden

Helen Wenley and Grace Haden

First published in 2015.

Copyright 2015 Unleashed Ventures Limited

Photography by Helen Wenley

Wenley, Helen

Short Walks in Auckland – Best of Central

ISBN 978-0-9941126-5-1

Auckland (N.Z.) – Auckland, Guide Books, Travel/walks

For current rules and locations for off leash dog exercise areas, please refer to the Auckland Council website.

Map source: openstreetmap.org

Auckland Public Transport Buses and Trains information: www.maxx.co.nz

ABOUT AUCKLAND

New Zealand consists of two main islands with unimaginative names - the North Island and the South Island.

Auckland sits on an isthmus in the North Island between two harbours - Waitemata Harbour to the north and Manukau Harbour to the south. The population of Auckland is higher than any other New Zealand City - just over 1.4 million currently. It's still a small city on a global basis.

There have been many tourists who have thought that New Zealand was connected to Australia by a bridge and yet others like a relative of mine who admired the view from the Sky Tower over lunch and confused the Waitemata Harbour with Cook Strait (the waters between the North and South Island).

Auckland is a city with lots of green spaces and native bush. There are many walks within Auckland away from the hustle and bustle of city life. There are some areas that are so close to residential houses or city streets and yet, you could feel very isolated because of the surrounding native bush.

Short Walks in Auckland aims to get you closer to Auckland, to learn about the history, the people, the geography, the geology, the flora and fauna, historic places and many other surprises which even well-seasoned locals will be surprised to find.

We wish to encourage you to get out and about; to discover Auckland on foot, so that you can feel a real sense of belonging, appreciation and excitement about what this unique and diverse city has to offer.

THE BEST OF CENTRAL AUCKLAND

These twelve urban walks have been chosen to showcase the beauty of Auckland's central area. You can enjoy the stunning views across the Hauraki Gulf, visit waterways and wetlands, explore the lush native bush, historical and volcano sites, as you walk from the central business district on the Waitemata Harbour to Onehunga on the Manukau Harbour.

Central Auckland has an extensive menu of walks (we currently have over 30 walks documented) and it is very difficult choosing a limited number to showcase. Although we have called these walks the "Best of", we enjoy all our short walks and we hope that you will too. We have endeavored to provide a diverse sampling to give you a taste of what Central Auckland has to offer. Please be aware that some of these walks also appear in our other books.

Once you have done these walks, you may wish to explore more of Central Auckland, another Auckland area and/or head further north, south, east or west for more challenging walks.

We wish to encourage you to get out and about; to discover Auckland on foot, so that you can feel a real sense of belonging, appreciation and excitement about what this unique and diverse city has to offer.

Download further maps and information:
Department of Conservation: *www.doc.govt.nz Parks & Recreation/Tracks&Walks/Auckland.*
Auckland Council:
www.aucklandcouncil.govt.nz/EN/parksfacilities/walkingtracks/Pages/home.aspx
Walking New Zealand Magazine: *www.walkingnewzealand.co.nz*

Getting Started...

Wear comfortable shoes to avoid sore feet (in winter prepare for mud and puddles).

Take water to sip, especially on hot summer days, for you and your dog.

Use sunscreen even on cloudy days.

Build up slowly if it's been a while since you exercised (take rest stops – most times you will find a park bench, and remember it's not a race!)

Walk with a 4 legged and/or human companion.

Why short circular walks?

We appreciate that many of you have busy lives, and do not have the time to head out of Auckland to spend a whole day walking. These walks have been compiled to help you explore and learn about your local area in small bites. If as a family you choose to do these walks with young children, then we hope that the walk's brevity will inspire them to continue walking and walk further when they become adults, as well as provide happy family memories.

The circular concept allows you the freedom to start the walk at any point along the route. Once you are familiar with the route, you can change it around by extending it, shortening it and of course walking in the reverse direction. You could even become creative and link one circular walk to another nearby circular walk.

We have documented over 100 short circular walks in Auckland. You can download individual walk self-guide brochures from our website: *www.walksinauckland.com*

CONTENTS

1. POINT ERIN AND HARBOURSIDE
St Marys Bay

This walk not only has fabulous views of Auckland's Waitemata Harbour, it is mostly flat (apart from the steep steps at "Jacob's Ladder" (which have in recent years been shortened)), Victoria Park has a great children's playground and skate park, and there are beautiful old homes to enjoy. There is also a dog off leash area along the way. Victoria Park Markets have recently been refurbished.

Enjoy the walk along the Westhaven Promenade beside the harbour with its marina, and the homes above in Saint Mary's Bay that look out over the harbour. Linger in Point Erin Reserve, or park up for a coffee at the Sitting Duck Café or stop at one of the viewing spots along the Westhaven Promenade.

Victoria Park Market: By 1900, sixty years after the first European settlers had arrived; Auckland had become New Zealand's largest and fastest growing city. However as Auckland grew, so too, did its rubbish. Following fears of bubonic plague, exacerbated by a plague outbreak in Sydney Australia, the City Council began work in 1904 on (what sounds, in retrospect like the name for a comic book hero) The Destructor; Auckland's first rubbish depot, situated in the then, working class suburb of Freemans Bay. Read more at www.victoria-park-market.co.nz

Nearby Walks:

Wynyard Quarter and Viaduct Harbour
Victoria Park to Western Park

Nearby Attractions: Harbour Bridge Climb, Victoria Park Markets, Erin Point Pools.

Description: A mix of level paths, one lot of steep steps. Suitable for users of average fitness and mobility. Running shoes suitable.

To see: Auckland City views, Rangitoto Island views, harbour views, Harbour Bridge.

Time: approx. 60 minutes. (about 5.4 kms)

Parking: Carparks in Westhaven Drive

Buses: Victoria Park Markets

Cafés: Various in Victoria Park markets, Sitting Duck Café.

Public toilets: Westhaven Drive, Victoria Park.

Children's playgrounds: Victoria Park, Point Erin.

Dogs: On leash, off leash at Point Erin.

Picnic Sites: Tables in Victoria Park and Point Erin, harbour side seats.

Directions:

Start from Victoria Park Market (car travelers' start from car park in Westhaven Drive #19).

1. Cross at the pedestrian lights towards the children's playground.
2. Go left < along Victoria Street.
3. Turn right > into Victoria Park just after the viaduct.
4. Turn left < towards the skate park.
5. Turn left < under the viaduct and walk alongside the carpark.
6. Cross Beaumont Street at the lights, on the other side, continue straight ahead up the ramp.
7. Turn left < up the steps (Jacob's Ladder).
8. Turn right > into Waitemata Street.
9. Turn right > into New Street.
10. Turn left < into London Street.
11. Cross St Mary's Bay Road and continue straight ahead into Hackett Street.
12. Turn right > into Shelly Beach Road.
13. Cross Shelly Beach Road at the traffic island just before Sarsfield Street (on the left).
14. Cross Sarsfield Street and turn left <.
15. Enter Point Erin Park on the path on the right > (off leash dog exercise area).
16. Near the approach to the road, turn left < to exit the Park into Sarsfield Street.
17. Turn right > into Sarsfield Street, cross over Curran Street and turn right >.
18. Go straight ahead, under the Harbour Bridge, then turn > right into Westhaven Drive.
19. At the Sitting Duck Café end of Westhaven Drive, follow the

Westhaven Promenade heading towards the city.

20. At the left hand bend on Westhaven Drive turn right > and head towards the traffic lights on the corner of Beaumont Street and Fanshaw Street.

21. Cross Fanshaw Street and then Beaumont Street at the lights, turn right > onto pathway in Victoria Park.

22. Turn left < at junction underneath viaduct.

23. Turn right > at Halsey Street and continue along footpath.

24. Turn left <, then right > towards the playground.

25. Just before the playground exit left < into Victoria Street and then right > along the footpath.

2. PARNELL MARKETS & RESERVES

Parnell is Auckland's charming, historic shopping village. It was established in 1841 and is Auckland's first suburb. Parnell is a tourist mecca and a thriving centre for creative businesses. The shops are unique and there are abundant cafes and restaurants. Parnell has access to various parks and reserves—the Auckland Domain, the Parnell Rose Garden, Scarborough Reserve and Alberon Reserve. Source: *www.parnell.net.nz*

We walk from the busy bustling markets to the peacefulness of reserves with birdlife, nikau palms and New Zealand native ferns, past quaint cottages and the massive Holy Trinity Cathedral and the more modest St John the Baptist Church.

This is a great walk if you wish to take in both markets on a Saturday or you can exclude them if you prefer a quieter walk. Dog friendly with off-leash exercise areas.

Parnell Village is a popular shopping strip with many cafes and restaurants to choose from. To make this a full day outing, you may wish to stay and explore Parnell Village and learn about its history. Visit *www.parnell.net.nz – visiting Parnell* for information.

Nearby Attractions:

Parnell Holy Trinity Cathedral, Parnell Rose Garden, Auckland Museum

Description: A mix of level paths and steep paths/steps. **Caution:** Muddy and slippery when wet. Suitable for most ages and levels of fitness and mobility, designed with flat shoes or running shoes in mind. Not suitable for wheelchairs and pushchairs.

To see: NZ native ferns palms and cycads, Waitemata Harbour views, farmers markets, old cottages.

Time: approx. 45 minutes. (about 3.92kms)

Cafés: la Cigale @ 69 St Georges Bay Road, Rosehip Café @ 82 Gladstone Road

Public toilets: In Parnell Road north of Denby Street

Children's playgrounds: None

Dogs: Off leash exercise areas

Picnic Site: Pick your favourite spot for your picnic rug. There are large picnic tables in Scarborough Reserve.

Directions:

Start from the Staffa Street (off Stratford Street) entrance.

1. Enter Alberon Reserve from Staffa Street.
2. Turn right > onto the boardwalk – nikau palms and ferns.
3. Turn right > at next junction.
4. Turn right > at concrete steps.
5. Turn left < after the steps then keep following the path and keep to the right.
6. Follow the concrete path thru reserve and turn right > at the junction (dog off-leash exercise area).
7. At the end of the reserve, turn left < into St Georges Bay Road
8. Come out of St Georges Bay Rd, turn left < then cross over Parnell Road at the lights and turn left < along Parnell Road.
9. Cross over Burwood Crescent and Claybrook Road, contunue straight ahead.
10. Turn right > into Domain Drive.
11. Turn left < into Titoke Street to visit Farmers Market (open Saturdays 8am to 12 noon).
12. Retrace steps to Domain Drive, cross the Drive and turn left <.
13. Turn right > into Forest Walk/Domain Walk.
14. Keep right > at the junction.
15. At the next junction follow the Domain Walk to Parnell down the steps to the   right >.
16. Turn right > at the next junction to Parnell via Railway Underpass and Ngahere Terrace.
17. Down at the railway track turn left < towards rail yards and then a quick right > to the Parnell Walk sign.
18. Go up the steps and at the top of the steps go straight ahead (centre fork) up the slight hill (Gibraltar Crescent).

19. Back onto Parnell Road, cross over at the pedestrian crossing on your left < and keep to the left–hand side of St John the Baptist church into Denby Street.

20. At the end of Denby Street turn right > and then immediately left < down the brick paved lane into Scarborough Reserve (dog off leash exercise area and large picnic tables).

21. Turn left < at the exit of Scarborough Reserve.

22. Then right > into the carpark (La Cigale cafe). French Farmers markets are held here every Saturday and Sunday morning.

23. From the front Carpark - keep the building and shed on your left <.

24. At the end, keep following building around to the left <.

25. Turn left < at the wooden boardwalk into Alberon Reserve, go up steps.

26. Straight ahead the turn left < at the steps and proceed down the steps.

27. Turn right > at end of the path back into Stratford Street.

28. For the nearest café turn left < into Gladstone Road, to the Rosehip Café at #82.

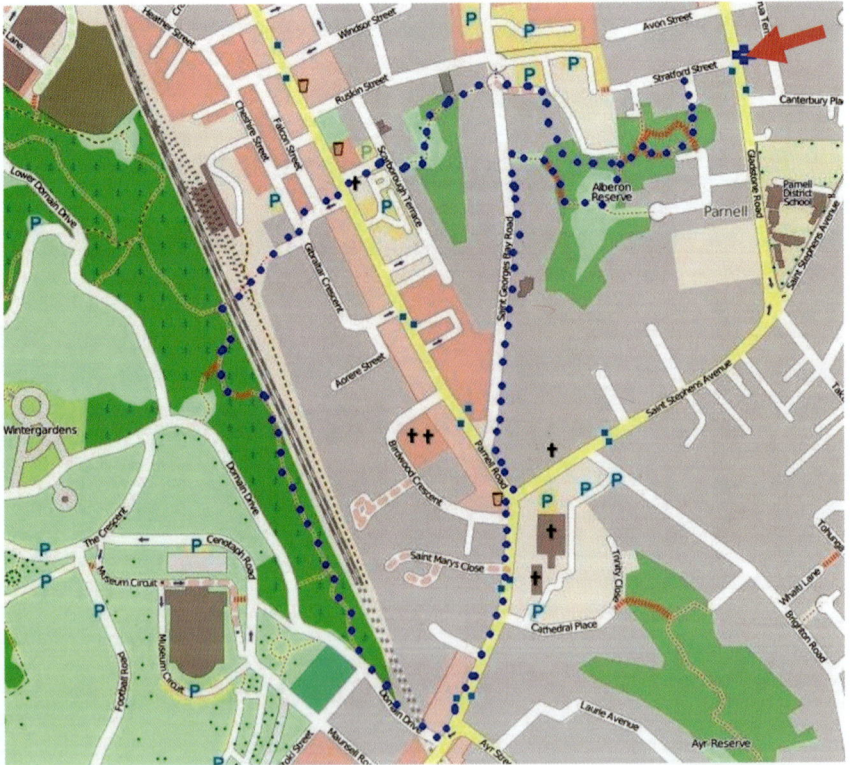

3. BRITOMART TO AUCKLAND MUSEUM

One day, we met a couple from California who were trying to find their way to walk to the Auckland Museum from the city. So thanks to them, we have documented this walk!

We decided to start the walk at Britomart, but of course, you can start walking from any point along the loop.

This mini-tour walk takes in the "old" parts of Auckland - the Auckland Domain, Albert Park (beside Auckland Art Gallery), Queen Street, Chancery Lane, Vulcan Lane, High Street, and old Government House.

The Domain itself is a beautiful place to stop and take a look around – there are the Wintergardens, duck ponds, statues. Take a picnic and choose a large tree to sit underneath. Or have lunch at the café.

The Museum is built on top of one side of the tuff ring of an extinct volcano (called Pukekaroro – hill of the black-backed gull). The height provides magnificent views of Waitemata Harbour and Rangitoto Island from the Museum steps. The duck ponds in the Domain are freshwater springs that emerge from the fractured scoria and lava fill in the crater.

This walk could be part of a whole day trip and include a visit to the Museum. Find out more: *www.aucklandmuseum.com*

Nearby Attractions: Auckland Art Gallery (Albert Park),

Description: A mix of level paths, steps and slightly inclined paths. Suitable for users of average fitness and mobility. May require boots in wet weather, running shoes suitable in dry weather.

To see: Auckland City views, Rangitoto Island view, City Lanes, Albert Park, Old Government House, Auckland Domain, Wintergardens, Museum

Time: approx. 60 minutes. (about 5.6 kms)

Parking: Start walk from the Auckland Museum

Cafés: Café Columbus Auckland Museum, Wintergarden Café Auckland Domain

Public toilets: Auckland Domain

Children's playgrounds: none

Dogs: On leash only

Picnic Sites: Seats only in Albert Park, Auckland Domain

Directions:

Start from Britomart or Auckland Museum (#11).

1. Turn left < from Britomart and cross Customs Street to the bottom of Queen Street.

2. Turn left < into Vulcan Lane, cross over High Street and then turn right > into O'Connell Street

3. Turn left < into Courthouse Lane, exit up the steps to the right >

4. Turn right > into Kitchener Street, then left < into Albert Park. Take the path to the left < at the fork.

5. Turn left < into Bowen Avenue.

6. Cross Princes Street at the corner lights, then enter the grounds of old Government House through the white gates on the corner.

7. Exit on the corner of Waterloo Quadrant and Symonds Street. Cross Symonds Street and continue straight ahead down Alten Road on the left hand side.

8. Cross Stanley Street at the lights and continue straight ahead down Alten Road to Carlaw Park Avenue.

9. Turn right > into Carlaw Park Avenue and proceed up the steps in Auckland Domain, follow the path to the right.

10. Follow the tar sealed road to the right > and at the next junction, turn left < up Lower Domain Drive.

11. Turn right > into Domain Drive, then left < into The Crescent, and then make your way to the Museum entrance.

12. On leaving the Museum, turn left < into The Crescent and walk towards the carpark, toilets and Duck Pond (near the Wintergardens and Kiosk)

13. Cross over Domain Drive and follow "Forest Walk – Centennial Walkway to Downtown Auckland" to Grafton Mews.

14. Cross over Grafton Road at the traffic lights and continue up Grafton Road past the Business School on your right.

15. Cross Symonds Street at the lights and continue up Grafton Road past the Maidment Theatre on your left.

16. Turn right > into Princes Street and cross over at the pedestrian crossing near the Clock Tower, to Albert Park.

17. Take the next path to the right >, and then the next left <

18. Turn left < into Kitchener Street, then right > into High Street.

19. Cross Shortland Street into Jean Batten Place. Turn left < into Fort Street, then right > into Queen Street.

20. Continue down Queen Street to return to the start.

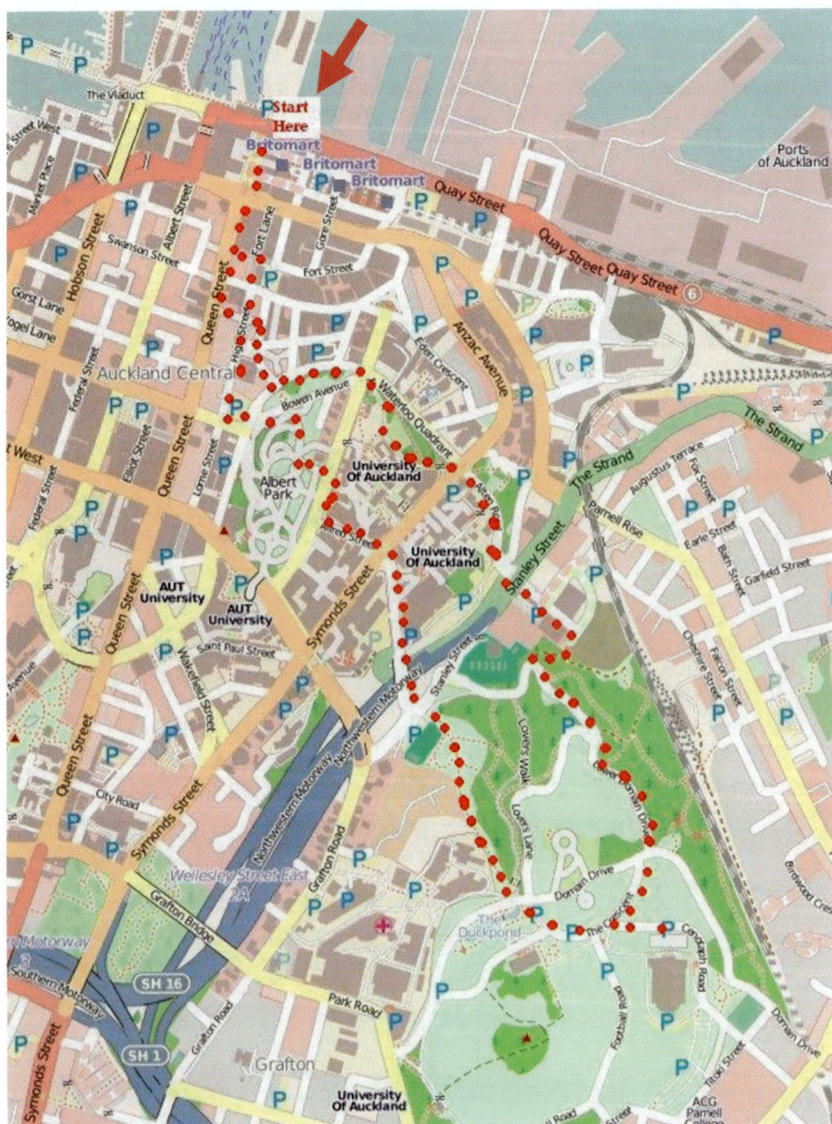

4. NEWMARKET TO HOBSON BAY

This walk is slightly longer than our usual, taking 90 minutes to cover just under 7.5kms. The route starts from the Railway Station in bustling Newmarket and moves along to the more sedate Remuera.

From the ridge of Remuera, we head down to the edge of Hobson Bay walkway, onto a boardwalk amongst the mangroves via parks, reserves, boardwalks, bush, residential streets and the Remuera mansions.

Waiata Reserve is tucked in between Victoria Avenue and Orakei Road - a beautiful large space, with magnificent trees- and is a dog friendly off-leash exercise area.

You may decide to explore the Remuera shopping centre on the way, or stop for a picnic in Waiata Reserve, or sit and enjoy the peace at Hobson Bay foreshore. And if you are including the walk as part of a day trip, you could spend a few hours exploring Newmarket.

Remuera: Long before the Europeans arrived, Remu-wera was probably the Maori name of an area near Mt Hobson, situated in Tamaki-Makau-Rau, on the isthmus between the Waitemata and Manukau harbours. The name Remu-wera comes from two words: remu meaning edge or hem, and wera meaning burnt.

Hobson Bay: Named after William Hobson – New Zealand's first governor – this bay is a tidal inlet. In the 1920s new transport routes were built to improve access to eastern Auckland with a train line going to Meadowbank.
Heritage walks brochures are available at the Remuera Community Library free of charge.
Martyn Wilson Fields — History is detailed at the corner of the reserve at Orakei Road entrance.

Nearby Attractions: Remuera (shops and cafes, restaurants), Orakei Basin (another off leash dog exercise area).

Description: A mix of level paths, steps and slightly inclined paths. Suitable for users of average fitness and mobility. May require boots in wet weather, running shoes suitable in dry weather.

To see: Volcano Views, shore birds, residential housing, mangroves, boardwalk, Mount Hobson

Time: approx. 90 minutes. (about 7.25 kms)

Start: Newmarket Train Station or Victoria Ave (start at #7 in the directions)

Cafés: Various in Newmarket and Remuera

Public toilets: Newmarket Park, Thomas Bloodworth Park

Children's playgrounds: Newmarket Park and Thomas Bloodworth Park

Dogs: Off leash dog exercise areas in Newmarket Park, Waiata Reserve, Bloodworth Park

Picnic Sites: Waiata Reserve, Thomas Bloodworth Park

Directions:

Start from Newmarket Railway Station.

1. Exit Newmarket Railway Station at Remuera Road/Nuffield Street and turn left < along Remuera Road.

2. Cross Remuera Road at the lights at the junction with Middleton Road, then turn left < along Remuera Road.

3. Cross Perry Street and continue up the sloping footpath straight ahead. Then continue up the steps that are straight ahead. (If you wish to go to the summit take the path to the right and then return).

4. Cross over Market Road, and then Remuera Road at the traffic lights.

5. Continue down Remuera Road.

6. Turn left < into Victoria Avenue.

7. Turn right > into Waiata Avenue.

8. Enter Waiata Reserve and follow the pathway.

9. Turn left < at the bottom of the hill and follow the path round to the right >.

10. Turn left < into Coombes Road.

11. Turn right > into Victoria Avenue, then cross Victoria Avenue to turn left < into Glenbrook Street.

12. Turn right > at the end of Glenbrook Street into Spencer Street.

13. Turn left < into Ingram Road.

14. Turn right > into Portland Road.

15. Opposite #189 Portland Road, cross over Portland Road to the small bridge. Cross the bridge and follow the path to the right >.

16. Cross over Shore Road and continue straight ahead on the path the swings to the right.

17. Turn right > onto the boardwalk.

18. Continue straight ahead after crossing the bridge, and keep

going until you reach steps – continue up the steps.

19. Turn left < and enter Ayr Reserve to the right, at the branch take the hard left < up the steps.

20. Turn left < at the T-junction.

21. Turn right > up the steps just before the roadway.

22. Cross over Ayr Street into Newmarket Park.

23. Turn left < at the playground and follow the path, turn left < at the pond and continue down the hill to the gully

24. At the culvert, continue up the steps straight ahead.

25. Turn left < at the end of the gravel path into James Cook Crescent.

26. Turn right > into the walkway that runs alongside #24 James Cook Crescent.

27. Cross over Joseph Banks Terrace to the ramp on the other side. Continue up the ramp to return to Newmarket Railway Station.

5. MOUNT EDEN (MAUNGAWHAU) & Village

Mount Eden

The most well-known, highest and probably most visited volcano in Auckland is Mount Eden.

It has a well-preserved deep crater and a fabulous view looking out to the city sky line, Waitemata Harbour and Rangitoto Island. There is also a view down on the famous Eden Park – home ground of New Zealand's national rugby team.

This walk takes you from the Mount Eden Village streets, climbing up to the summit, a loop around the water reservoir, down the other side, into a dog off-leash area and a children's playground (with a flying fox), then round the base on the western side back to Mount Eden Village.

Friends of Maungawhau have kept up with planting native trees, so that over time, the mountain will have improved heritage protection.

The village of Mount Eden at the base of the mountain has a mix of cafes, restaurants and small shops.

History:
Maungawhau (the Maori name for Mount Eden) is named after the whau tree, one of the world's lightest woods which was used for fishing floats and utility rafts. New cultivation techniques brought from the Pacific saw massive production of taro and kumara. Huge gardens spread from the base of Maungawhau through the modern day Mt Eden suburb with volcanic rocks used as passive solar heating for seed raising beds to help tropical crops adapt to the colder environment.

www.aucklandcity.govt.nz/whatson/places/walkways/mteden/early.asp
www.maungawhau.co.nz/resources/archaeology.html

Nearby Attractions:

Eden Gardens - www.edengarden.co.nz

Mt Eden Village - www.mounteden.co.nz

Heritage walks brochure –
www.aucklandcity.govt.nz/whatson/places/walkways/mteden/pdf/

Description: A mix of level paths and steep paths/steps. Suitable for users of average fitness and mobility. May require boots in wet weather, running shoes suitable in dry weather.

Caution: Muddy and slippery when wet.

To see: Volcano crater, Auckland City views, Waitemata Harbour views and the Waitakere Hills.

Time: approx. 60 minutes (about 4.74 kms).

Parking: Owens Road (off Stokes Road/Mt Eden Road)

Buses: ASB Bank Mt Eden Village

Cafés: Various in Mt Eden village

Public toilets: Stokes Road, Normandy Road and Mt Eden Road (near Tahaki Reserve)

Children's playgrounds: Normandy Road

Dogs: Off- and on-leash areas

Picnic Sites: Tables in playground area and Tahaki reserve

Directions:

Start from between #117 & #113 Owens Road (Stokes Road) off Mt Eden Road.

1. Head up the steps. Go thru the gate and take the steps to the right >. Continue on path up the hill.

2. Go through the gate and turn left < at the road (stay clear of vehicles coming from behind you). Views looking south – Eden Park the home ground of the All Blacks Rugby team.

3. Turn right > along the road to the summit (enjoy the view of Auckland City on your left). Follow the pathway around the crater. (Past the lookout points on your right).

4. Turn right > down gravel path (post with yellow marker).

5. Optional: At the flat water reservoir area on left, follow path the around in a loop to look at view, then return to main path.

6. Turn left < down the   road.

7. At the steps on the left <, follow the paved footpath path down the hill.

8. At the gate at the roundabout, take a hard right <; keep the Sky Tower straight ahead and cross the stile.

9. Take the path straight ahead that goes down the hill (Off-leash dog area).

10. Cross the stile over the wire fence, turn right > and go down the stone steps.

11. At the reserve/childrens playground (NB public toilets here), take the paved path on the left < (beside the flying fox) up to Tahiki Reserve.

12. Cross the entrance to carpark to the path on the other side.

13. Take path on the left < up the steps.

14. Turn left < at the top of the steps (signpost Clive Road).

15. Take the next turn right > along the footpath and follow the main path.

16. Turn right > at the end of the path.

17. After a short distance, cross over at the junction and go thru the gate on right > (beside the summit road and the carpark) and then turn right > just before the end of the small concrete patch.

18. Continue straight ahead on grassy track, keep left < at the forks, stay on uphill paths.

19. Continue straight ahead.

20. Keep left < at junction where the path broadens.

21. At the gate, follow path around to the left, then continue straight ahead.

22. Take the right > fork.

23. Turn hard right > at next junction and go down the steps.

24. Exit thru the gate turning right > and follow the Rautangi Road back to Mt Eden Road.

25. Turn left < into Mt Eden Road and walk back thru Mt Eden Village.

6. ONE TREE HILL – MAUNGAKIEKE

Epsom

Cornwall Park/One Tree Hill Domain is highly developed with a road and footpaths around the volcano and up to the summit. This walk takes you from the children's playground at the Manukau Road entrance around the western side to visit the summit and/or view the crater, then into Cornwall Park, past the visitor's centre and restaurant returning on the eastern side through Twin Oak Drive and then following the road overlooking Manukau Harbour with a view across to Mangere Mountain. The paths are wheel-friendly though there are some inclines.

One Tree Hill is one of the largest volcanic cones in the Auckland region. It erupted more than 20,000 years ago. The lava from the eruption flowed along old stream valleys south down to Onehunga.

Cornwall Park/One Tree Hill Domain was donated to the people of Auckland by Sir John Logan Campbell (he is buried on the top of One Tree Hill). Cornwall Park is named after the Duke and Duchess of Cornwall and York (who later became King George V and Queen Mary of England).

It is also a large city farm park. It contains a sheep and cattle farm, an observatory, BBQ picnic areas, a children's playground, an archery club, a cafe, and an ice-cream kiosk.

This is a place to come to enjoy the change in seasons, (especially spring when the new lambs and calves are born; and the daffodils, magnolias, and cherry trees are in bloom) and to spend a whole day. There are many more paths to explore.

The nearby village of Greenwoods Corner has a variety of shops where you can purchase picnic and BBQ food.

Facilities: Flying fox, pergola, tables, drinking fountains, bike stands, Skate Park.
Visit the information kiosk for a selection of brochures and to watch a film.

History: *www.cornwallpark.co.nz*

Nearby Attractions:
Auckland Stardome Observatory *www.stardome.org.nz*
Royal Oak Mall
Greenwoods Corner Village (Pah Road/Manukau Rd)

Description: A mix of mainly level paths, and a few steep paths. Suitable for users of all ages and abilities, suitable for normal footwear and for wheelchairs and pushchairs.

To see: City views, harbour views, trees, volcano, farm animals, and observatory. The Park is home to many birds ranging from Native Pigeon, Fantail to California quail, White-faced Heron and Paradise Shelduck.

Time: approx. 60 minutes. (about 5.14kms)

Start: Carpark, Manukau Road entrance.

Cafés: 1) Frolic Café, Manukau Road opposite the park entrance. I have had many coffees here – children friendly.

2) Cornwall Park Restaurant and ice-cream kiosk

3) Various at Greenwoods Corner (Golf Road exit).

Public toilets: Manukau Road Carpark, beside the Cornwall Park Restaurant and near the Archery Club.

Children's playgrounds: Beside the Manukau Road entrance. Lots of paths for children to ride bicycles near the band rotunda.

Dogs: On leash area only

Picnic and Barbecue facilities available.

Directions:

Start from the carpark (entrance Manukau Road between Lewin Road and Haydn Avenue).

1. Take the footpath to the left < of the playground keeping the observatory on your right > as you head up the hill.

2. Keep left < past the Sorrento Conference Centre (do not turn right).

3. Follow the road on the right > to the summit (may be omitted if too steep).

4. Follow the road back down the hill and turn right > to continue around the hill (passing alongside the Olive Grove).

5. Proceed past Acacia Cottage on the left < and the Information Centre and restaurant on the right >. Visitors may wish to visit the Information Centre.

6. Continue down the hill keeping to the path between the trees.

7. Continue past the picnic area, toilets and carpark.

8. Take the next right > and follow the fence line around to the left <.

9. Cross over Pohutukawa Road at the pedestrian crossing and continue along paved walkway. Take the right > fork.

10. Follow the walkway to the bandstand.

11. Turn right > at the bandstand, follow the walkway to the carpark. Cross the carpark and follow the one-way road to the roundabout.

12. Turn left < at the roundabout into Twin Oak Drive. (Watch out for families of pheasants feeding under the oak trees.)

*** see *Optional Excursion.*

13. Follow the road along the path until you reach the Sorrento Conference Centre.

14. Turn left < and follow either the road or the path down the hill and back to the carpark and children's playground.

*** *Optional Excursion*:

13. At the next right-hand bend cross over the road, and follow the road (Grand Drive) to the right > that has a picnic area beside it.

14. Follow the road until you reach a small wooden gate, on the right > in front of a stand of trees.

15. Enter the area and note the ferns and volcanic rocks (and if you are very quiet children might see some "magic fairies"!).

16. Walk through and out the other side - exit from the gate in the corner (opposite the archery club and toilets).

17. Follow the road along the path until you reach the Sorrento Conference Centre.

18. Turn left < and follow either the road or the path down the hill and back to the carpark and children's playground.

7. ONEHUNGA TO PAH HOMESTEAD

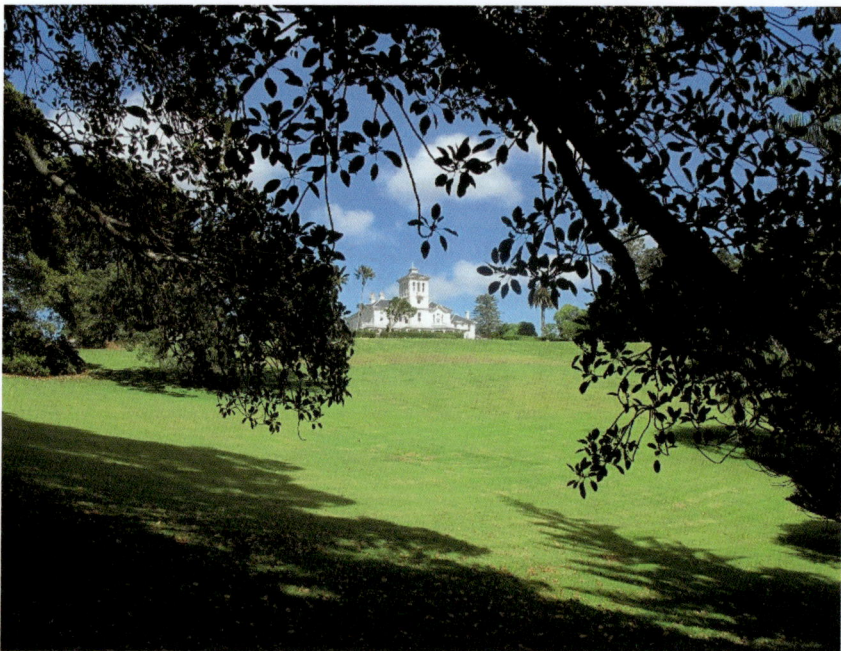

This walk provides several options if you wish to make it part of an exploration. The Onehunga Railway station is a great spot to arrive in Onehunga at the southern end of the mall.   From here you can amble slowly and enjoy the curious collection of shops, seek out some of Onehunga's landmarks or just push on up the hill.

Once you reach Monte Cecilia Park you can enjoy the magnificent old trees and the views across to One Tree Hill and Mangere Mountain, before heading down to Onehunga Bay Reserve. Or you can linger longer and walk around Pah Homestead and view the art collection at the TSB Bank Wallace Arts Centre

This walk takes in 3 children's playgrounds and numerous cafes. Catch the train to Onehunga and consider making this into a day outing by taking the time to discover the places of interest along the way. Onehunga Heritage Walk: *onehunga.net.nz/manukau-heritage-walk-onehunga.* And for shoppers, Dressmart Outlet Shopping offers a large range of products.

Onehunga was one of New Zealand's first and busiest ports. In the 1840's attractive Government legislation allowed settlers to buy land direct from Maori land owners on payment of a small tax to the government. Onehunga was seen as a key position in the military and naval defence of the perimeter of Auckland and thus became one of the areas for Fencible settlement. (Fencibles were from the military pensioners and discharged soldiers in Great Britain. They would be known as 'The Royal New Zealand Fencibles' also referred to as Pensioners and were to become permanent settlers as well as a back-up military force.)
More information at: *onehunga.net.nz*

Other Attractions:

TSB Bank Wallace Arts Centre, Pah Homestead.

Description: A mix of level paths, steps and slightly inclined paths. Suitable for users of average fitness and mobility. May require boots in wet weather, running shoes suitable in dry weather.

To see: Historic cottages, Views of One Tree Hill and Mangere Mountain, Historic Homestead and parkland

Time: approx. 90 minutes. (about 7.5 kms)

Start: Princes Street Onehunga

Cafés: The Library Cafe and Columbus Coffee

Public toilets: Onehunga Mall, Onehunga Bay reserve

Children's playgrounds: Jellicoe park, Onehunga Bay Reserve

Dogs: On leash only

Picnic sites: Jellicoe Park, Monte Cecilia Park, Onehunga Bay Reserve

Directions:

Start from Onehunga Railway Station, Princes Street.

1. Exit right > into Onehunga Mall and head north.

2. Turn left < into Trafalgar Street.

3. Turn left < into Selwyn Street.

4. Turn right > into Grey Street.

5. Turn right > into Jellicoe Park.

6. Cross over Queenstown/Pah Roads and turn right >.

7. Turn left < into Korma Road.

8. Turn left < Monte Cecilia Park (Korma Road entrance) and continue straight ahead up the paved path alongside the metal fence (Marcellin College grounds).

9. Turn left < at cross paths and follow gravel path to the TSB Bank Wallace Arts Centre.

10. At next junction turn left < along the Carriage Way Walk (or turn right > to enter the Pah Homestead for the TSB Bank Wallace Arts Centre).

11. At the T junction, turn right > and retrace your steps back to Korma Road.

12. Turn right > into Korma Road.

13. Turn right > into Pah Road.

14. Cross over Herd Road, then Queenstown Road at the lights, continue down the hill.

15. Turn left < into Beachcroft Avenue towards Onehunga.

16. Cross Beachcroft Avenue just past the pedestrian bridge (that goes over the motorway) and enter Onehunga Bay Reserve. Continue straight ahead alongside the lagoon.

17. Exit the via the car park and turn right > along Beachcroft Avenue.

18. Continue straight ahead into Princes Street.

19. Return to Onehunga Mall.

8. Big King (Te Tatua a Riukiuta)

Three Kings

This walk commences at the Duke Street entrance off Mt Eden Road. It is a popular walk for dog owners as it includes a dog off-leash exercise area. It explores the remains of the volcano, provides views of the city skyline and other volcanoes such as Mt Albert, Mt Roskill, Mt Eden, Mangere Mountain and Rangitoto Island. The route takes you down through the local residential area and children's playgrounds.

The Three Kings area is a volcanic centre formed 15,000 years ago when the 300 meter deep crater filled with lava and built three scoria mounds and overflowed into a 10 kilometer "river" through Western Springs to terminate as the Meola Reef in the Waitemata Harbour. The reserve has been planted with many pohutukawa trees that look magnificent when fully in flower.

In the period of Maori settlement it was a Pa site, evidence of this can still be seen on the western slopes.

The land was acquired by Governor Fitzroy in 1845 and in 1922 it was purchased by the current owners, Winstone Ltd. The area is now Auckland's largest scoria quarry which has resulted in a large pit, and leaves Big King, which was gifted to Mt Roskill Borough Council in 1927, as the only remaining cone. Big King remains as a council reserve and hosts a Watercare reservoir at the top. A further Watercare reservoir is concealed on the slopes.

The Three Kings panorama 1920 Big King is in the centre.   Courtesy of Auckland City Libraries

Wesleyan Missionary Society set up a Native Institution for training native teachers; this moved from Grafton to an 80 hectare farm and provided Christian education for young Maori and needy European children. It transferred to Paerata in the early 1920's; its former location is marked with a plaque on McCullough Ave.

Arthur S. Richards Memorial Park was formed during the late 1930's and the following decade as part of a major housing development by the State. The land was part of the site of the Wesley College and was declared Crown land in 1949; it is notable for its mature trees.

Nearby Attractions: Call in to Mount Eden Village on the way back to the city.

44

Description: A mix of level paths, steep paths and steps. Not wheel-friendly. Moderate fitness. Sturdy shoes recommended. Caution: Slippery and muddy when wet.

To see: Volcanoes, gravel pit, parks and playgrounds, 1960's state housing. Wonderful views of Manukau Harbour, South Head and the Waitakere Hills.

Time: approx. 45 minutes (about 3.45kms).

Parking: Main carpark off Duke Street (off Mt Eden Road)

Cafés: Orvietto, 935 Mt Eden Rd or The Eiffel, 985 Mt Eden Rd

Public toilets: by Duke Street carpark.

Children's playgrounds: Arthur Richards Memorial Park, Robertson Reserve (off Smallfield Ave)

Dogs: Off- and On-leash areas

Picnic Sites: Pick your favourite spot.

Directions:

Start from the carpark (Duke Street, Three Kings).

1. Follow the path straight ahead from the carpark.

2. At junction of 3 paths, take the lower path on left <.

3. Follow the path around to the right >.

4. Veer to the right > again.

5. Enjoy the view from the top of Big King beside the water tower.

6. Head back down the hill again, take the next left < and then right > at the T-junction. Follow the walkway alongside the quarry, heading south.

7. Turn right > at the bottom of the steps, keeping to the right > hand side of the playing field in the natural bowl, exiting up the grassy hill track on the right, just before reaching the corner.

8. Turn left < into Fyvie Ave.

9. Turn left < into Smallfield Avenue.

10. Turn right > into Robertson Reserve in between the school and the playground. Walk alongside the fence on the left < beside the school.

11. Turn right > at exit into McCullough Ave.

12. Turn left < into Scout Ave, then right > into Arthur Richards Memorial Park.

13. Turn hard right > and walk along the fence line "off-path", on the grass at the edge of the park behind the houses (the path straight ahead leads to the playground).

14. Turn right > at the corner to exit and turn right > into McCullough Ave.

15. Turn left < into Fyvie Ave, and then left < between #18 and #20 into Big King Reserve.

16. Turn hard left < at the next junction (before the water pipe on your right) and continue straight ahead.

17. Turn left < at the next junction (Big King on your right) and continue straight ahead.

18. Continue straight ahead at the cross paths.

19. Exit into Duke Street and turn right > to return to the car-park.

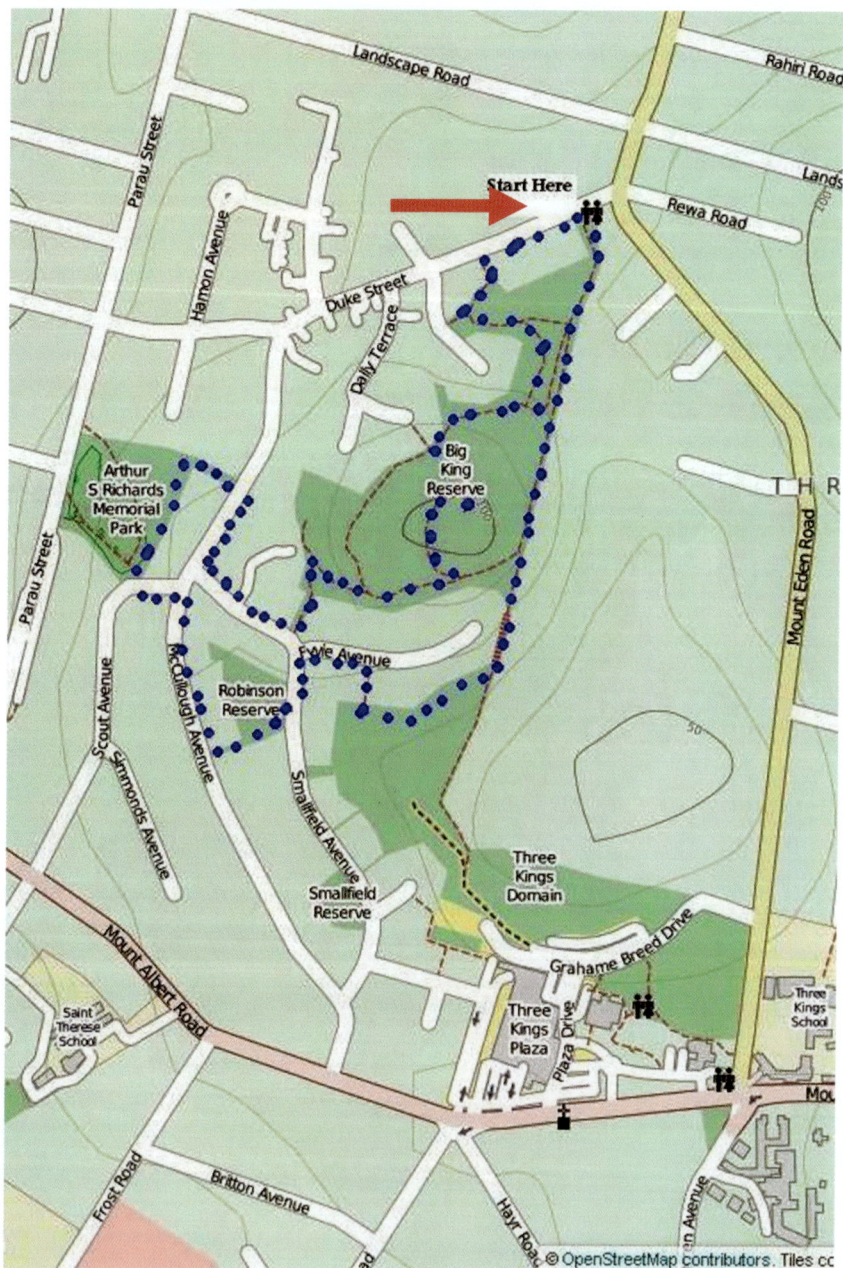

9. MOUNT ROSKILL

The volcano double cone and twin craters of Mt Roskill have been destroyed through the installation of a water reservoir, but from the top it is easy to view Mt Albert, Mt Eden, Big King and One Tree Hill. On a windy day you may see people flying kites on the top of Mt Roskill.

Our flat walk (if you choose not to walk up to the summit of Mt Roskill) links up three reserves - War Memorial Park, Walmsley Park and Underwood Park. Take some bread to feed the ducks in Oakley Creek, or stop and have a picnic along the walkway. The final part of the walk is at the Stoddard Road shops with windows filled with beautiful colourful saris.

Description: Mostly level paths, steep paths ascent to summit of Mt Roskill. Suitable for most ages and levels of fitness and mobility, designed with flat shoes or running shoes in mind. Suitable for wheelchairs and pushchairs if Mt Roskill summit is avoided.

To see: Views of Auckland City skyline, Mt Albert, Mt Eden, Three Kings, One Tree Hill. Oakley Creek and ducks.

Time: approx. 90 minutes (about 7.15 kms).

Start: Countdown carpark, Sandringham Road extension.

Cafés: Stoddard Road, and The Roskill Coffee Project @ 740 Sandringham Road

Public toilets: War Memorial Park

Children's playgrounds: War Memorial Park (May Rd & Sandringham Rd)

Dogs: Off leash areas: Walmsley Park and Underwood Park

Picnic Sites: In the reserves – take a rug.

Directions:

Start from the corner of Stoddard Road and Sandringham Road extension.

1. Follow the pathway towards the motorway and cross the pedestrian bridge over the motorway.
2. Turn left > and continue along the shared cycleway/path alongside the motorway.
3. Turn right > at Dominion Road to follow the road up to the summit of Mt Roskill. Return to this point.
4. Turn left < along Dominion Road and cross the motorway heading north.
5. Follow the footpath along Dominion Road.
6. Turn left < at Memorial Avenue.
7. Turn right > into May Road, cross at the pedestrian refuge, turn right > then left < into War Memorial Park.
8. Follow the path alongside Oakley Creek.
9. Cross Sandringham Road extension, turn right > then left > to enter Walmsley Park.
10. Continue straight ahead, cross Beagle Avenue into Underwood Park.
11. Turn left < into Richardson Road.
12. Keep left < to turn into Stoddard Road.
13. Cross Stoddard Road and continue left < to return to start.

10. OAKLEY CREEK

Waterview/Mt Albert

The Oakley Creek area has been rescued from potential destruction from roading, tunnels and housing. It is most famous for having the only waterfall (6 metres high) in central Auckland. We start our walk at the harbour edge at Heron Park before crossing into the reserve.

This walk explores the southern end of the reserve. At the time of this publication, Waterview Tunnel works is in progress, which has temporarily cut off the pathway around the mouth of Oakley Creek. The source of the Creek is in Hillsborough where it starts its 15 km journey via Mount Roskill and Mount Albert.

Heron Park is named after the white-faced heron (matuku moana) that nest in the pine trees.

The Creek has been restored and preserved by the Friends of Oakley Creek. Over 35,000 native plant species have been planted over recent years. The Creek is now a natural and beautiful reserve.

Visit www.oakleycreek.org.nz if you would like to help with the continual maintenance and restoration.

Nearby Walks:

Oakley Creek North (available when motorway tunnel works have been completed)
New Lynn Whau River Loop

Description: A mix of level paths, steps and slightly inclined paths. Suitable for users of average fitness and mobility. May require boots in wet weather, running shoes suitable in dry weather.
To see: Water birds Habitat, waterfall, Oakley Creek
Time: approx. 60 minutes. (about 4 kms)
Parking: Cadman Avenue (off Fairlands Avenue/ Great North Road)
Buses: Fairlands Avenue/ Great North Road

Cafes: None nearby
Public toilets: Heron Park
Children's playgrounds: Heron Park and Harbutt Reserve
Dogs: On leash with off leash areas in Harbutt Reserve, Phyllis Street Reserve and Heron Park
Picnic Sites: Seats and tables in Heron Park.

Directions:

Start from Cadman Avenue (off Fairlands Avenue/ Great North Road).

1. From the carpark area, turn right down the hill along the northern side of Heron Park.
2. Keep to the main path going straight ahead.
3. At the bridge turn right > and continue following the main path.
4. Cross Great North Road to Blockhouse Bay Road at the pedestrian lights.
5. Turn up Blockhouse Bay Road to the right >.
6. Turn left < into Cradock Street.
7. At the end, follow the sign to the Oakley Creek Walkway.
8. Cross the bridge at the bottom and turn left <.
9. Ignore the steps on the right (Harbutt Reserve entrance 1) and keep going straight ahead.
10. At the t-junction turn left < (Harbutt Reserve entrance 2 on right).
11. At the top of the steps turn left < and follow the fence line to the carpark.
12. At the carpark turn right > to exit Phyllis Street Reserve.
13. Cross Phyllis Street and continue straight ahead down Springleigh Avenue.
14. Turn left < into Laurel Street.
15. At the end of Laurel Street exit in the break of the stone wall and then the hedge.
16. Continue straight ahead through the carpark (Unitec).
17. At the road turn left < head towards Building 76.
18. Go around Building 76 and head to the Oakley Creek Walkway sign.

19. At the bottom of the path turn left < across the bridge then left < again on the other side.

20. Keep following the creek straight ahead.

21. Ignore the two paths on the left (Phyllis Reserve entrances), and continue straight ahead.

22. Turn left < from the reserve and cross Great North Road at the traffic lights.

23. Enter Heron Park and take the path straight ahead toward the children's playground.

24. Return to the start point.

11. WESTERN SPRINGS & MEOLA REEF (TE ARA WHAKAPEKAPEKA O RUARANGI)

Point Chevalier

We begin the walk beside Western Springs Park. We follow the path around the lake (look out for baby water birds from September to December) and then cross Motions Road to follow the path along the stream. We head past MOTAT to come out on Meola Road. From there we enter Meola Reef Reserve (a popular off-leash dog area). We do the loop and return via Jaggers Bush Reserve and back through Western Springs Park.

Western Springs Park is a sanctuary for both people and wildlife. It surrounds a natural spring-fed lake, one of Auckland's early water supplies.

Meola Reef is a lava flow that came from the Mt St John, Mt Eden, One Tree Hill and Three Kings volcanoes and was formed 15,000 years ago when the 300 meter deep crater filled with lava and overflowed in a 10 kilometer "river" through Western Springs to terminate as the Meola Reef in the Waitemata Harbour. It is the longest lava flow in the Auckland volcanic field. The area around the reef is a 15-hectare reserve with stands of mangrove and salt marsh. Underground and above ground streams from Mt Albert, Mt Eden and One Tree Hill feed into the Harbour at Meola Reef.

Nearby Attractions:
MOTAT (Museum of Transport and Technology)
Auckland Zoo

Description: Mainly level paths plus steps. Suitable for most ages and levels of fitness and mobility, designed with flat shoes or running shoes in mind. Not suitable for wheelchairs and pushchairs.

To see: Waitemata Harbour views, a natural spring-fed lake with ducks, swans, geese and long-finned eels; stream, trams, planes.

Time: approx. 90 minutes. (about 7kms). This walk can be shortened as required.

Parking: Great North Road (Western Springs Gardens) opposite Western Springs.

Buses: Great North Rd. opposite Motions Rd

Cafés: None close by. Walk/drive/bus up Great North Road to Point Chevalier village, or drive/bus to Kingsland or Kings Plant Barn (St Lukes Road) or Garnet Station café in Garnet Road.

Public toilets: Western Springs beside the children's playground, Meola Reef.

Children's playgrounds: Western Springs – near entrance to Zoo carpark.

Dogs: Off-leash areas available at Meola Reef and Jaggers Bush.

Picnic Sites: Western Springs - BBQ's & tables near children's playground.

Directions:

Start from the carpark in Great North Road.

1. Cross Great North Road to Western Springs Park.

2. Follow the path to the right > towards 'Stadium/MOTAT, lakeside walk'.

3. Turn right > at the lake edge.

4. Next junction turn left < and follow the lake edge all the way around until you reach the children's playground.

5. Straight ahead at the children's playground.

6. Exit at the Zoo's carpark and follow the exit road down to Motions Road.

7. Cross Motions Road to the other side (use the pedestrian island).

8. Turn left < then right > down the steps across the stream (Pasadena Walk).

9. Keep to the right-hand footpath and continue straight ahead, go past Pasadena Intermediate School.

10. Follow the path around the edge of school field (following stream).

11. At the end of the path cross the bridge and head back to Motions Road.

12. Turn left < and follow Motions Road past TAPAC.

13. On the corner at Western Springs College, continue straight ahead towards MOTAT.

14. Cross Meola Road to a carpark and a Meola Reef Reserve sign.

15. Turn left < and follow the footpath alongside Meola Road.

16. Take the path on your right > (which is on the left < of the car park - it's not obvious) that goes into trees (not towards the Meola Reef Reserve sign).

17. Turn left < at the T-junction.

18. Straight ahead past the toilet block.

19. Go through the gate into dog off-leash area.

20. Straight ahead follow the fence line.

21. At the end of the path, keep going straight ahead to the gate in the far corner of the fence.

22. Head left < towards the end of the Point (and a rubbish bin).

23. Optional loop at the tip of the Meola Reef Point (with view of Auckland Harbour Bridge).

24. Turn right > and follow the path beside the rubbish bin, keep going straight.

25. Turn left < at second turning (back to entrance).

26. Cross Meola Road, turn left <. (You may wish to catch the tram back to Western Springs).

27. Go past Seddon Fields entrance.

28. Turn right < into Jaggers Bush Reserve.

29. Follow the path straight ahead. After the bridge go up the steps to the left <.

30. Follow the footpath past Western Springs College and TAPAC.

31. Cross Motions Road at pedestrian lights, and go straight ahead up the slope to re-enter Zoo carpark.

32. Head to far corner of the carpark back to the entrance of Western Springs lakeside.

33. Turn right > at the corner of the playground.

34. Keep to the left < for Great North Road.

35. Turn right > after crossing the double arched bridge.

36. Cross Great North Road to return to carpark.

12. GREY LYNN

This walk explores both **Cox's Bay Reserve** and **Grey Lynn Park**. Cox's Bay Reserve is made up of three parks - Hukanui Reserve where the new boardwalk (opened 15th June 2013) is, Bayfield Park where you may wish to have your picnic, and the sports fields of Cox's Bay Park. It is a mini-paradise for dog owners with off-leash dog exercise areas.

And it is family friendly too, with a selection of children's playgrounds and picnic sites. It is a great place for joggers and people who like to use the outdoor fitness stations.

The wide open spaces, sculptures, playing fields, the creek, mangrove swamps, gullies, the bay itself, a field with cattle and tall mature trees surrounded by interesting residential housing, make this another walk that is full of variety.

Also of interest is the Kelmarna Gardens Nature Trail off Hukanui Crescent - A self-directed nature trail will show you chickens, vegetable gardens, a pony and young cattle, an organic orchard, beehives, worm farm, compost making, native trees and flax. The trail winds its way through the gardens, across paddocks and links to Cox's Creek Walkway. The gardens were established in 1981 and have been organically managed for 32 years. The land is owned by Auckland Council for the benefit of the whole community.

For history information visit "Meanderings about Cox's Creek".

Nearby Walks: Western Springs and Meola Creek

67

Description: Paved walkways, steps, inclines and board walks. Suitable for users of average fitness and mobility.

To see: Sculptures, playing fields, the creek, mangrove swamps, gullies, the bay itself, a field with cattle and tall mature trees surrounded by interesting residential housing.

Time: approx. 70 minutes. (about 5.58 kms)

Start: Westmoreland Street West off Richmond Road, Grey Lynn.

Cafés: Bread & Butter, 34 Westmoreland St. West

Public toilets: Grey Lynn Park

Children's playgrounds: Cox's Bay Reserve and Grey Lynn Park

Dogs: Off leash areas in Cox's Bay Reserve and Grey Lynn Park — check signage for rules.

Picnic sites: Cox's Bay Reserve and Grey Lynn Park

Directions:

Start from Westmoreland Street West, Grey Lynn (off Richmond Road).

1. Cross Richmond Road, turn right > and turn left < to enter the Cox's Creek Walkway opposite Westmoreland Street West.
2. Continue straight ahead until you reach a cross path junction.
3. Turn left < and follow the path around the playing field of Cox's Bay Park, past the changing sheds and toilets.
4. Turn right > alongside West End Road with a view of Cox's Bay.
5. Follow the walkway straight ahead back around the other side of the playing fields.
6. At the cross path junction turn left < and cross the bridge into Bayfield Park.
7. Turn right > at the next junction and cross another bridge.
8. Continue straight ahead into Hukanui Crescent.
9. Continue straight ahead along Parawai Crescent.
10. Take the next left < into Tawariki Street (signposted to Moira Reserve).
11. At the very end of Tawariki Street, turn right > into the walkway beside #41.
12. Cross over Moira Street, continue straight ahead.
13. Turn left < into Richmond Road, then cross over at the pedestrian crossing, continue left <.
14. Turn right > into Farrar Street. Cross Jessel and Cockburn Streets.
15. Enter Grey Lynn Park at the very end of Farrar Street.
16. Continue straight ahead until you reach a 4 way junction and the entrance to "The Grey Lynn Sculpture Park".
17. Enter the gully "Sculptura", and continue straight ahead.
18. Take the left < path to Rose Road and follow the road around

the corner to the right > into Arnold Street.

19. Re-enter Grey Lynn Park via the Arnold Street entrance.
20. Continue straight ahead at the junction and follow the path past the basketball hoops and public toilets.
21. Turn right > into Dryden Street.
22. Turn left < into Cockburn Street, cross the road, turn left <.
23. Turn right > into the Cox's Creek Walkway (between #58 & #33).
24. Take the left < fork, cross Sackville Street, turn left < along Sackville Street.
25. Turn right > into walkway between #27a and the pensioner flats.
26. Turn left < into Westmoreland Street West and follow the road to the right > to return to the start.

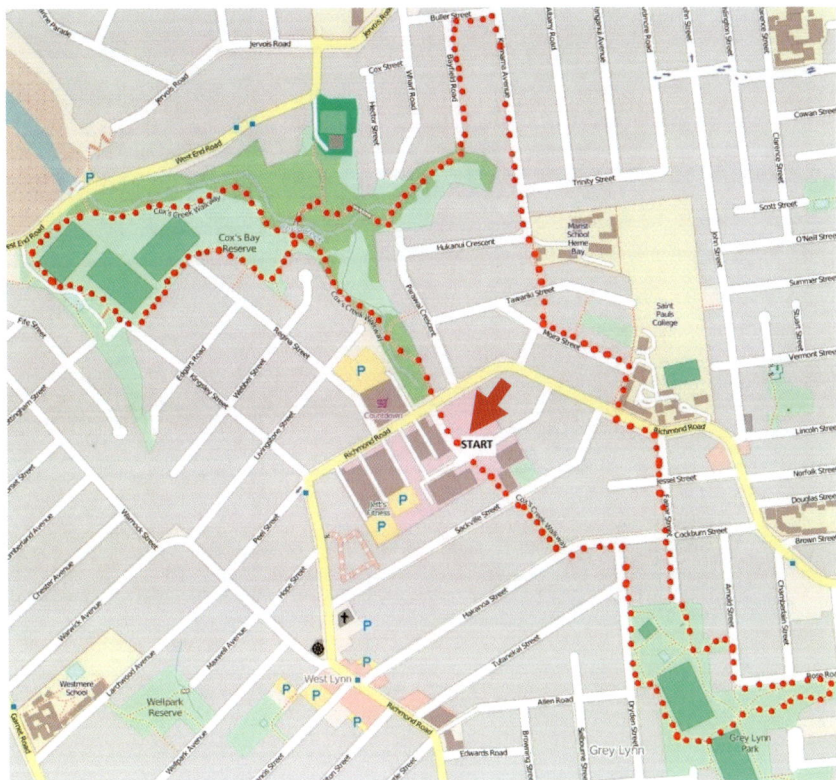

RESOURCES for dog owners.

Auckland Council – current dog regulations:
aucklandcouncil.govt.nz/EN/licencesregulations/dogsandanimals/
Pages/home.aspx

Please be aware that off leash dog exercise areas are subject to change.

Dog friendly web sites:
doogle.co.nz
fetchmag.co.nz
planmyplay.co.nz/spotlight/auckland-special-interest-dog-friendly-exercise-areas-beaches
localist.co.nz/auckland/articles/top-10-auckland-dog-parks

Dog friendly beaches and other areas. Please check Auckland Council website and signage for current regulations.

1. Takapuna, Cheltenham and North Head on the North Shore.
2. Kakamatua on Manukau Harbour.
3. Kauri Point on the North Shore.
4. Mission Bay and Kohimarama along Tamaki Drive.
5. Mellons Bay near Howick.
6. Taipari Strand, Taikata Road, Te Atatu Peninsula.
7. Waikowhai Park off Hillsborough Road

ABOUT THE AUTHORS

For many years, Helen and her friend Grace talked as they walked around Cornwall Park and One Tree Hill. One day, Grace turned to Helen and said "Would you like a change from walking around here?" Helen replied "Yes, but where would we go?"

And that was the beginning of the Mini Adventures for Maximum Enjoyment – for Health, Fitness and Fun. Grace scouted out the routes, the girls would get lost at times, but they walked on. And then Grace bought herself a smart phone and even though they still got lost, they could tell where they were from the map on the phone.

The walks had to comply with strict criteria – first of all, they had to be circular, each walk had to provide interest and a 'wow' factor, if there was a café nearby even better. But most of all, they had to be fun and enjoyable – not tedious.

The walks in this book have all been traversed (more than once) by Helen and Grace (and documented by Helen) so that the walker has very little chance of getting lost.

"Short Walks in Auckland website has been brilliant find for Sport Waitakere as we are both working towards a common goal."

Emma Haigh | Active Communities Advisor |

Sport Waitakere

On behalf of The University of Auckland, I would like to thank Helen for the custom route maps she has produced for our popular 'Walk the Talk' programme. The maps are perfect for our needs, professionally made and well received by participants.

Hugh Markham, Active Recreation Manager,

The University of Auckland

More walk guides available at

www.walksinauckland.co.nz

WHAT WALKERS ARE SAYING...

The thing I enjoy most about walking in Auckland is the variety. There are so many choices and you can have completely different surroundings on each walk.

The things we like most of walking in Auckland. - Auckland's diverse landscapes (beaches, bush, volcanoes and urban) offer superb variations to suit all ages, weather and abilities. We have beautiful spots to see, never too far from a coffee or lunch and get the added benefit of healthy exercise.

All the lovely diverse views, hills, trees and parks, native bush, beach and sea side places

I enjoy the diversity of walks in Auckland, from bush walks to waterfront walks, heritage walks to walks through suburban streets, parks and cafes! There are always lots of new things to discover and explore.

This year we moved from the Netherlands to Auckland. Walking is a very good and pleasant way to explore our new home country. Short Walks in Auckland is a good help.

Walking with family, variation i.e. coastal, forest, volcanoes.

Being able to take in the vast variety of sights sounds and smells, Flora and Fauna, and its varying landscape.

I enjoy going for walks on Auckland's volcanoes, I have on occasions done a different volcano every day for a week or two with people who are recovering from mental illness and they found this very beneficial. Thank you for your very informative e-mails and walking guides.

The best thing about walking in Auckland is the variety, city walks, volcano walks, park walks, harbour walks, etc and you can never know what the weather will throw at you

As a fairly newly retired person, it is a great source of pleasure to me to have the time to walk. Living in west Auckland there are many options and varieties to choose from. However, I particularly enjoy the walks around Te Atatu Peninsula that give views of the city, quiet bird sanctuaries through coastal estuaries and there is always somebody to say hello to.

CURRENT TITLES IN THIS SERIES

Volcanoes
Coastal Walks (part one)
Coastal Walks (part two)
Urban Bush
Dog Friendly Walks (part one)
Dog Friendly Walks (part two)
Dog Friendly Walks (part three)
Best of the West
Best of the East
Best of the South
Best of the North

Available from Amazon.com and Auckland Libraries

Printed in Great Britain
by Amazon

13207259R00048